BUTTERFLY PAINTINGS

by

Sue Wright Owens

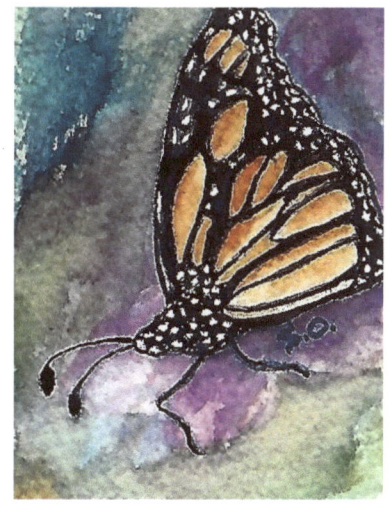

Watercolor and poetry Copyright © 2018 by Sue Wright Owens. All rights reserved. Printed in the United States of America. No part of this book may be used or reproduced in any manner whatsoever without written permission, except in the case of brief quotations embodied in critical articles and reviews.

ISBN 10: 172344460X
ISBN 13: 978-1723444609

Introduction

For years, I have been fascinated by butterflies. Thirty-six years ago I began classes in watercolor and during my first two years in class I painted the butterflies that are on this book cover.

Throughout the years I have read several books about butterflies and I have grown milkweed plants for Monarchs, which led to my observing chrysalis and the emerging butterfly.

In 1993 our youngest son sent me a butterfly garden for my birthday. In the kit was a clear plastic container with five worms in it. Who else would think to send five worms to their mother for her birthday! I spent about two weeks observing the complete cycle of the Painted Lady butterfly. This was a wonderful experience and one that I documented each day with illustrations and comment.

In addition to these butterfly paintings and illustrations I have painted and given away 12 miniatures , 8 special flower/butterfly paintings for my high school 50th reunion classmates and 16 special cards with butterflies.

I mourn the devastating impact which modern farming and development practices have rendered these beautiful creatures and pray that they can survive the evolutionary process and not be lost.

I am in total awe when I look through butterfly books and see the many different kinds and colors. Our God was certainly busy and quite and artist!!

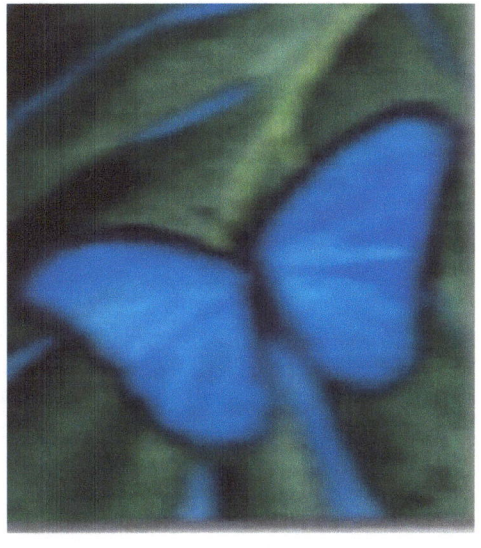

BRIEF ENCOUNTER

Oh lovely, fragile butterfly,
your presence is so fleeting.
I see you as you flutter by.
You're in a rush this evening.

And now, you've stopped to rest a while,
to pause there on a flower.
I slowly move and then I smile
and hope you'll stay an hour.

Your quick departure to the air
fills me with disappointment.
I wanted so to stand and stare
for longer than a moment.

But you've important things to do,
so many plants to visit.
I'm thankful for a glimpse of you.
Your beauty is exquisite.

What is a butterfly? At best he's but a caterpillar dressed.
  Benjamin Franklin

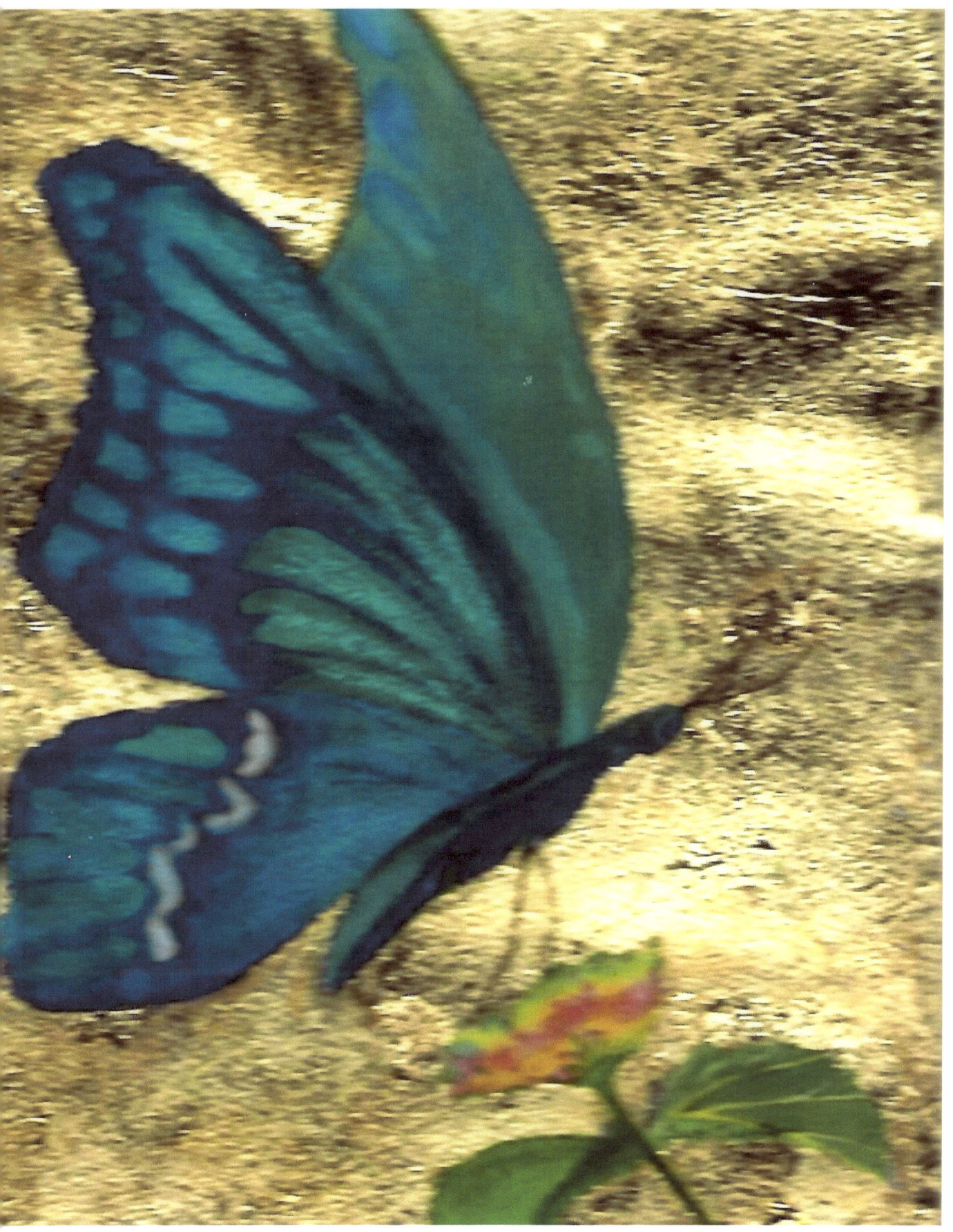

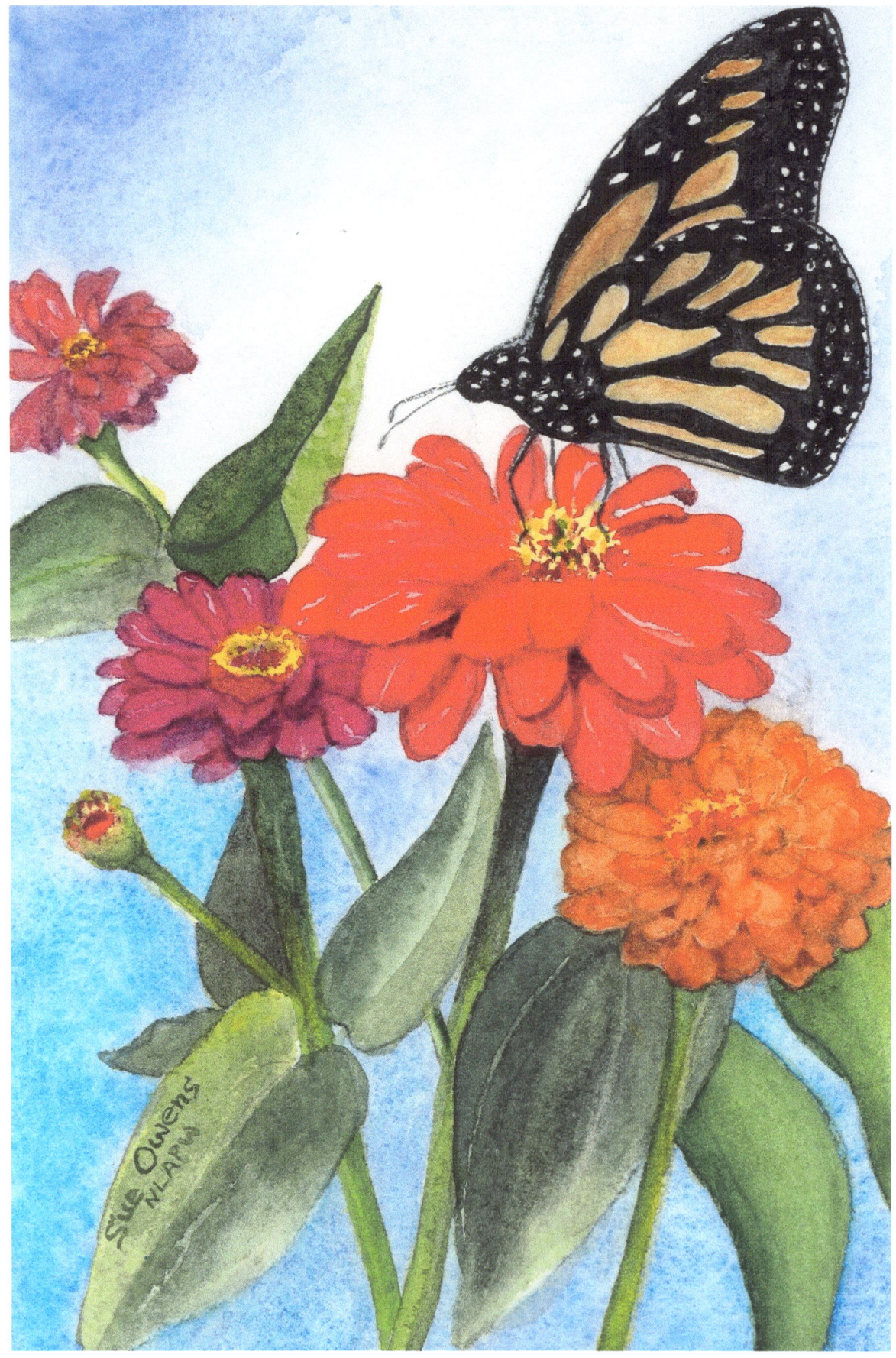

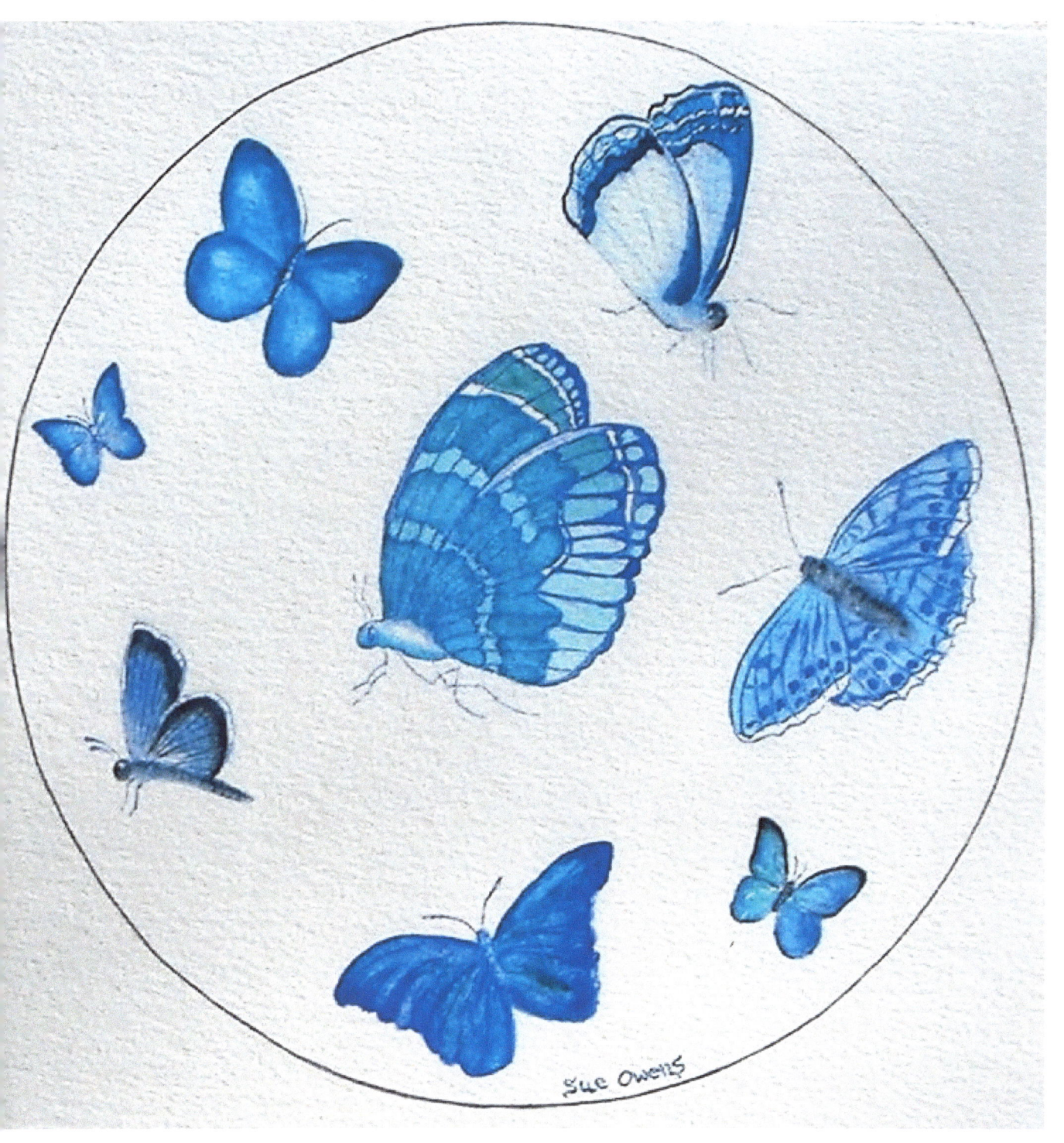

Paper Plate Design

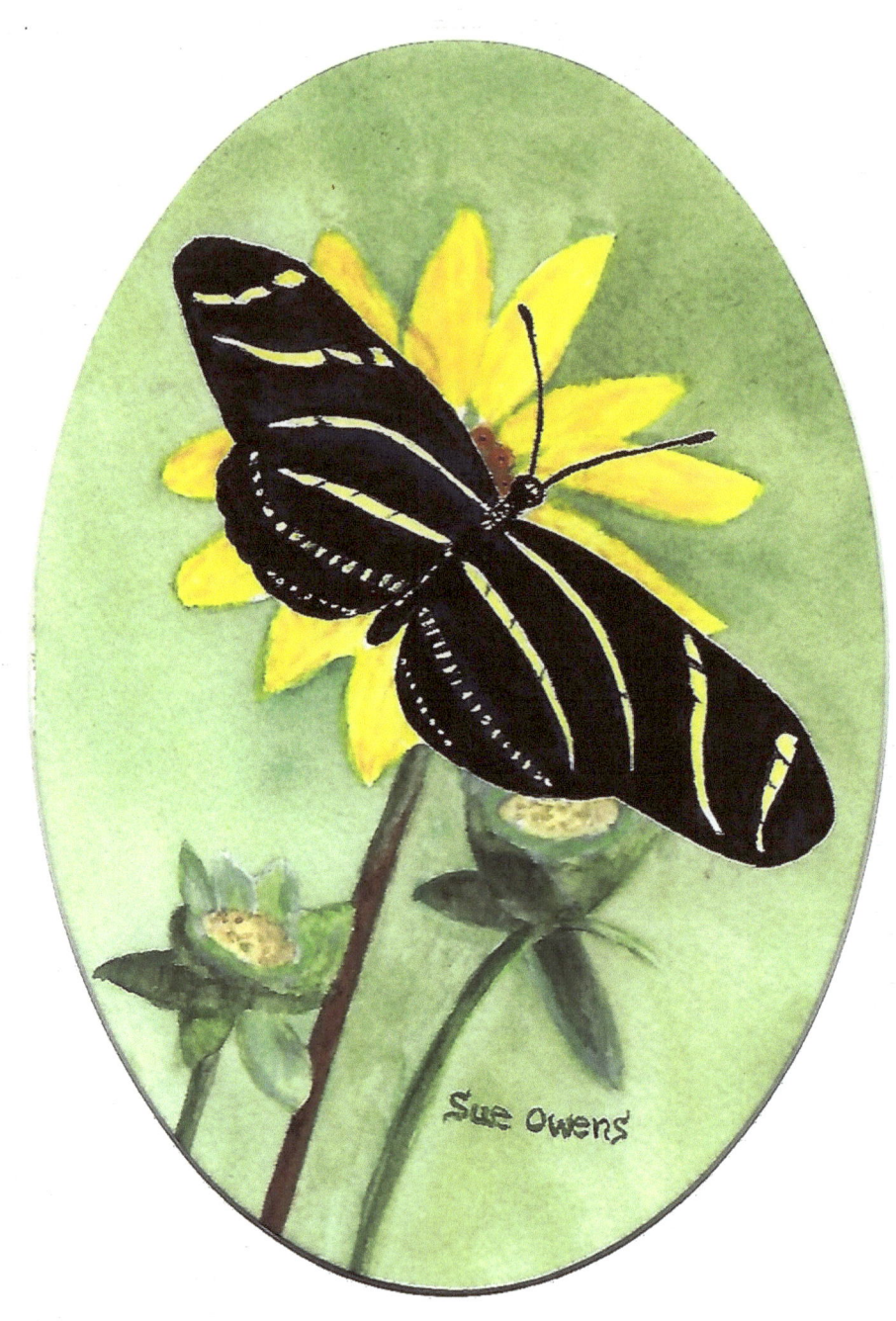

Zebra Longwing on Yellow Daisy

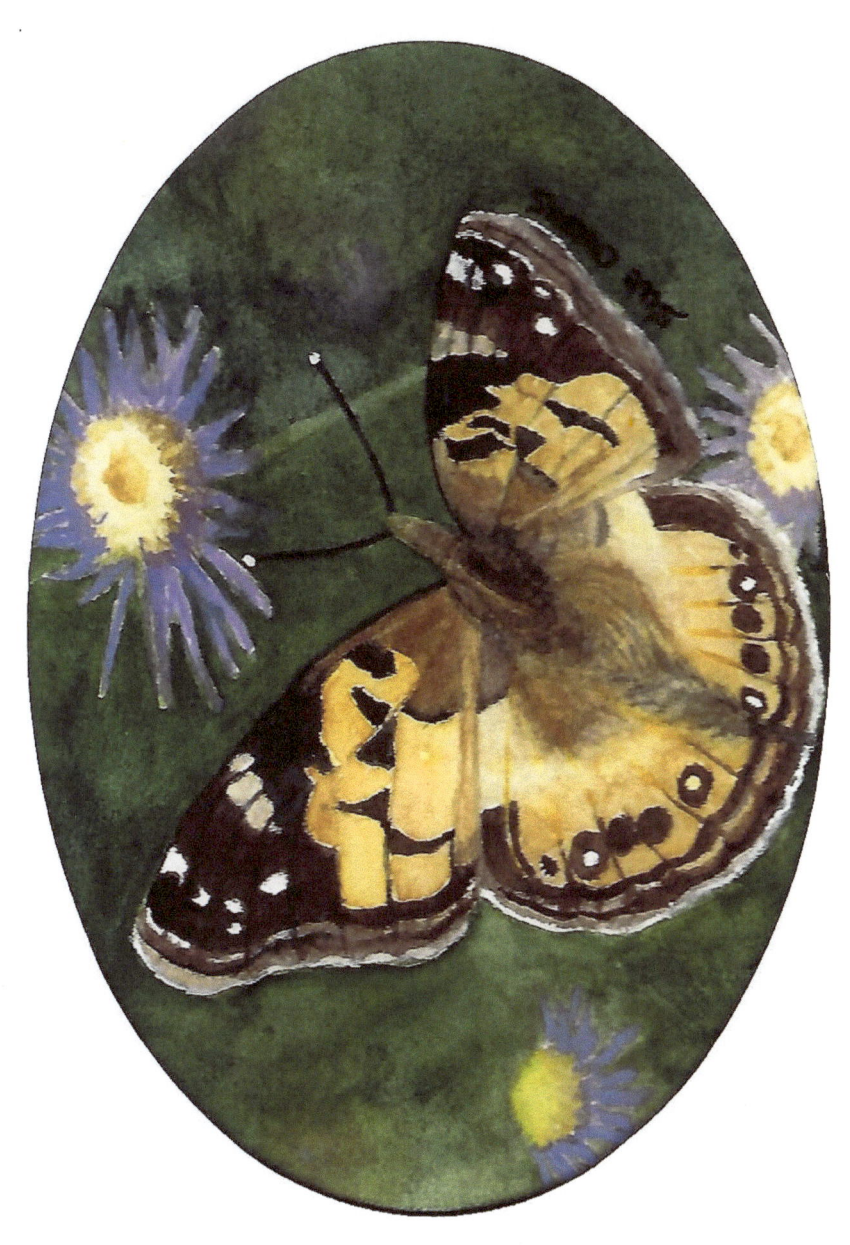

Painted Lady on Asters

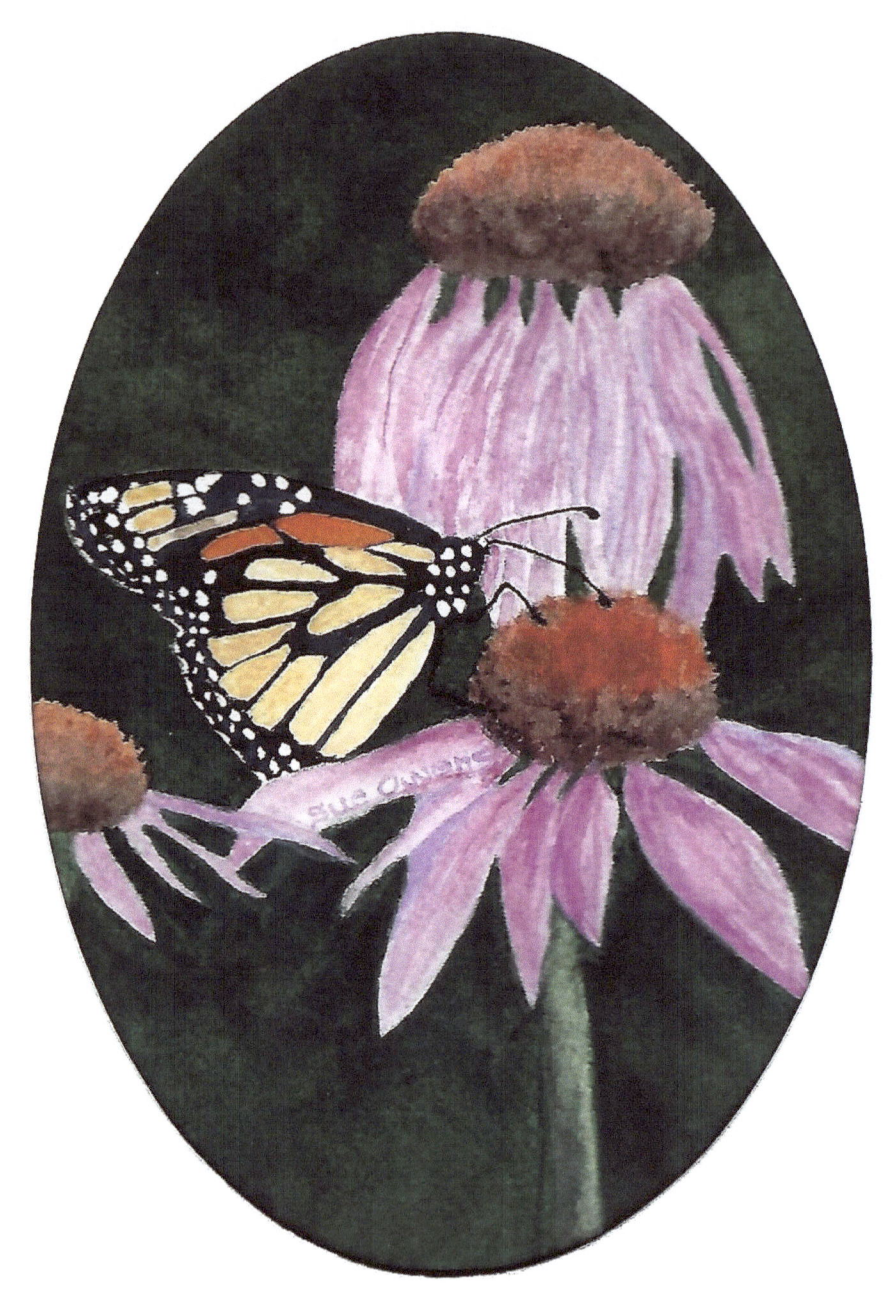

Monarch Butterfly on Cone Flower

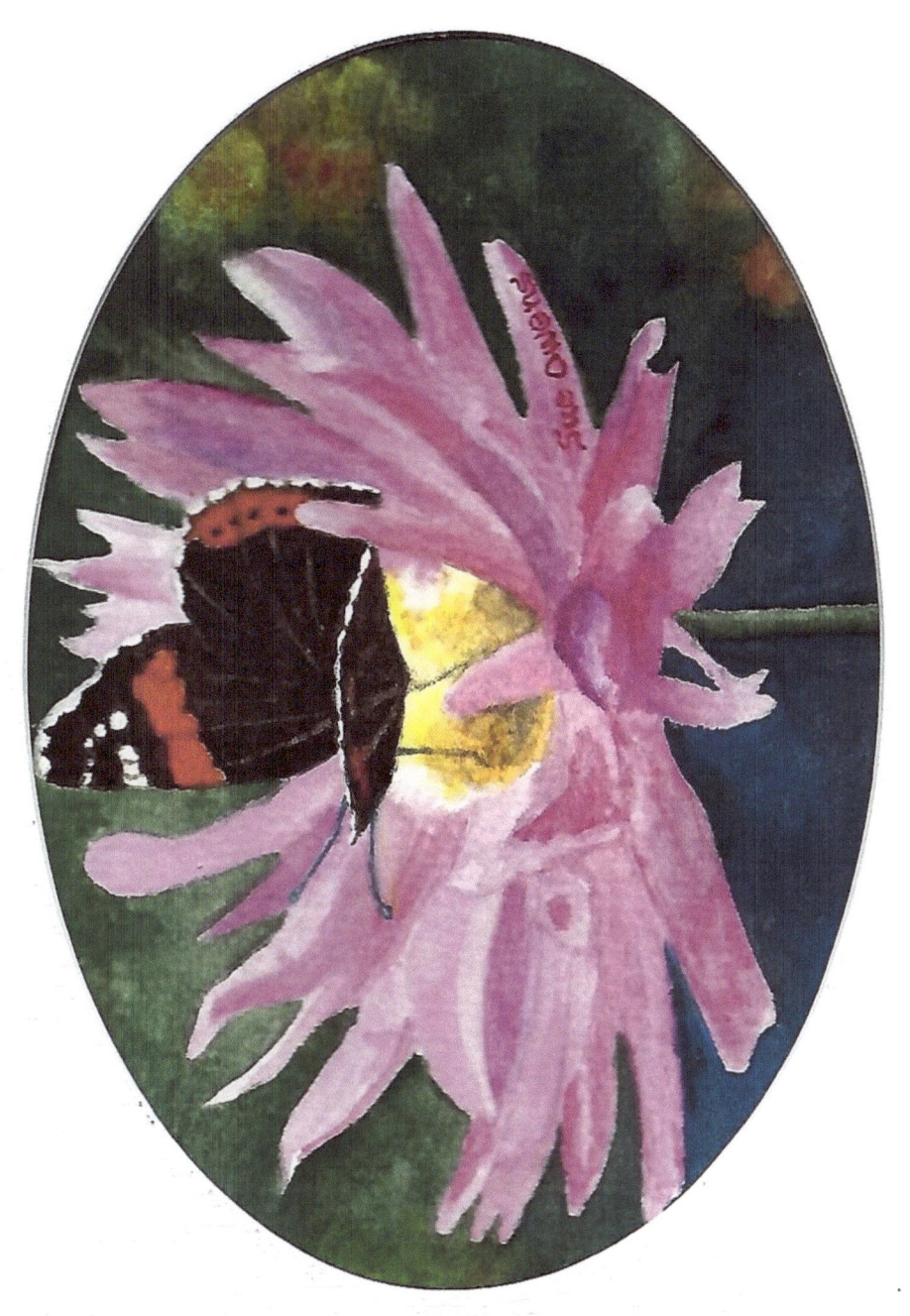

Red Admiral Butterfly on Zinia

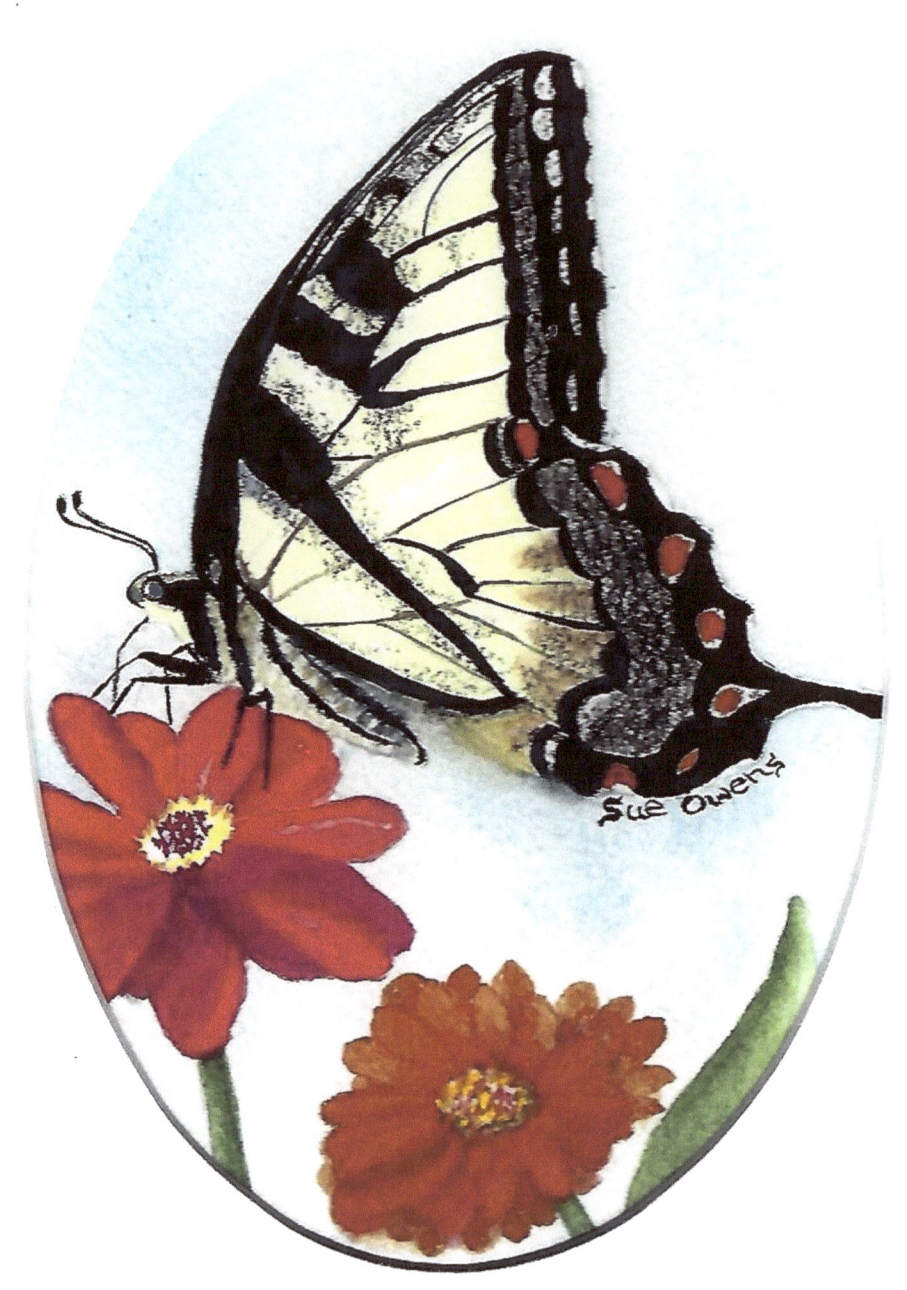

Eastern Tiger Swallowtail

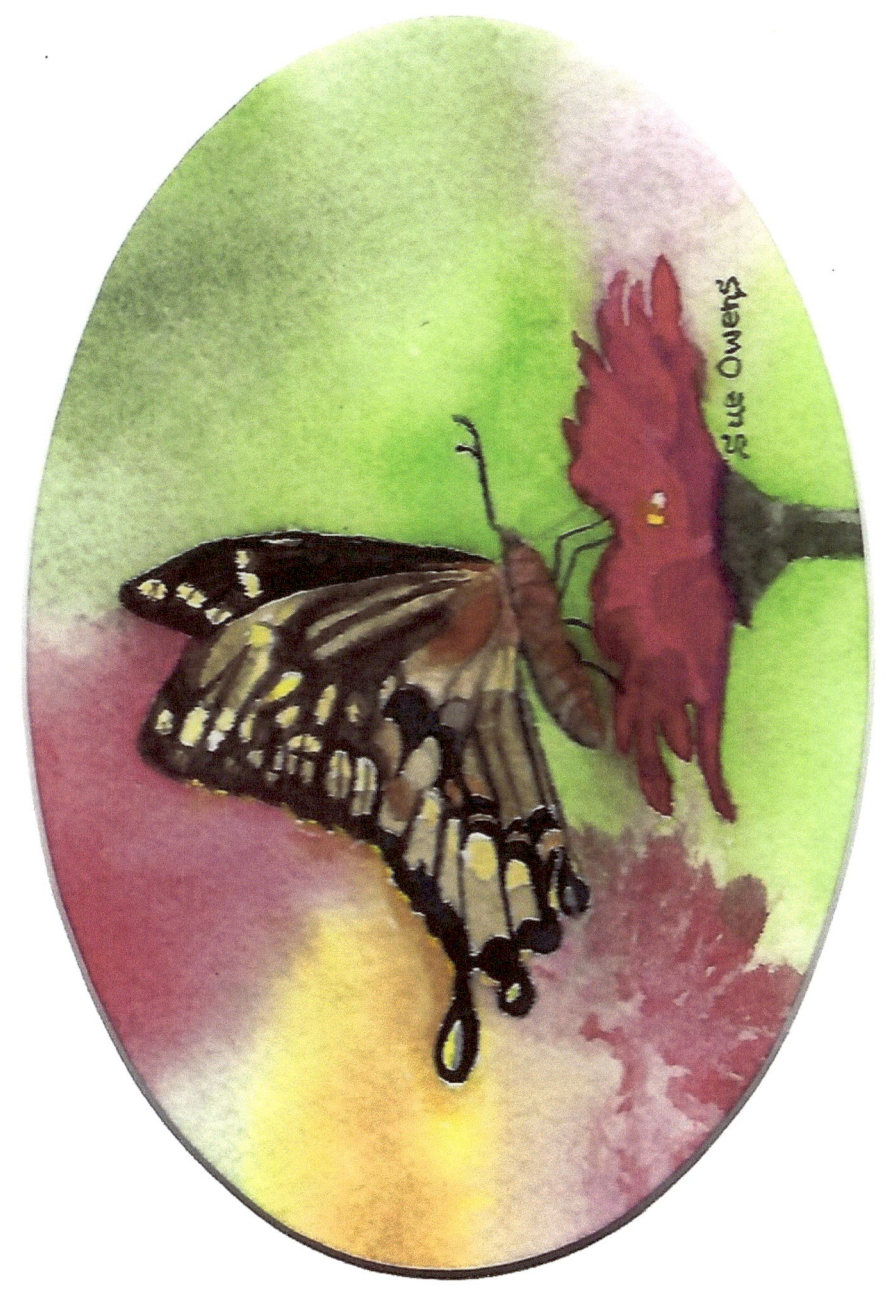

Giant Swallowtail on Zinia

A STORY

ABOUT

A

BIRTHDAY PRESENT

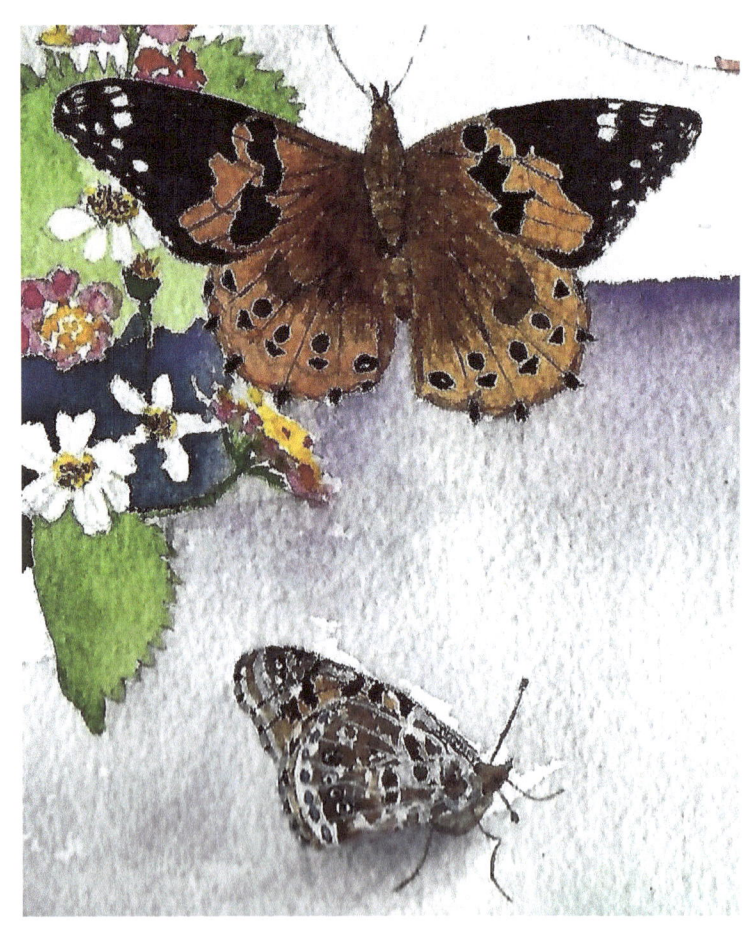

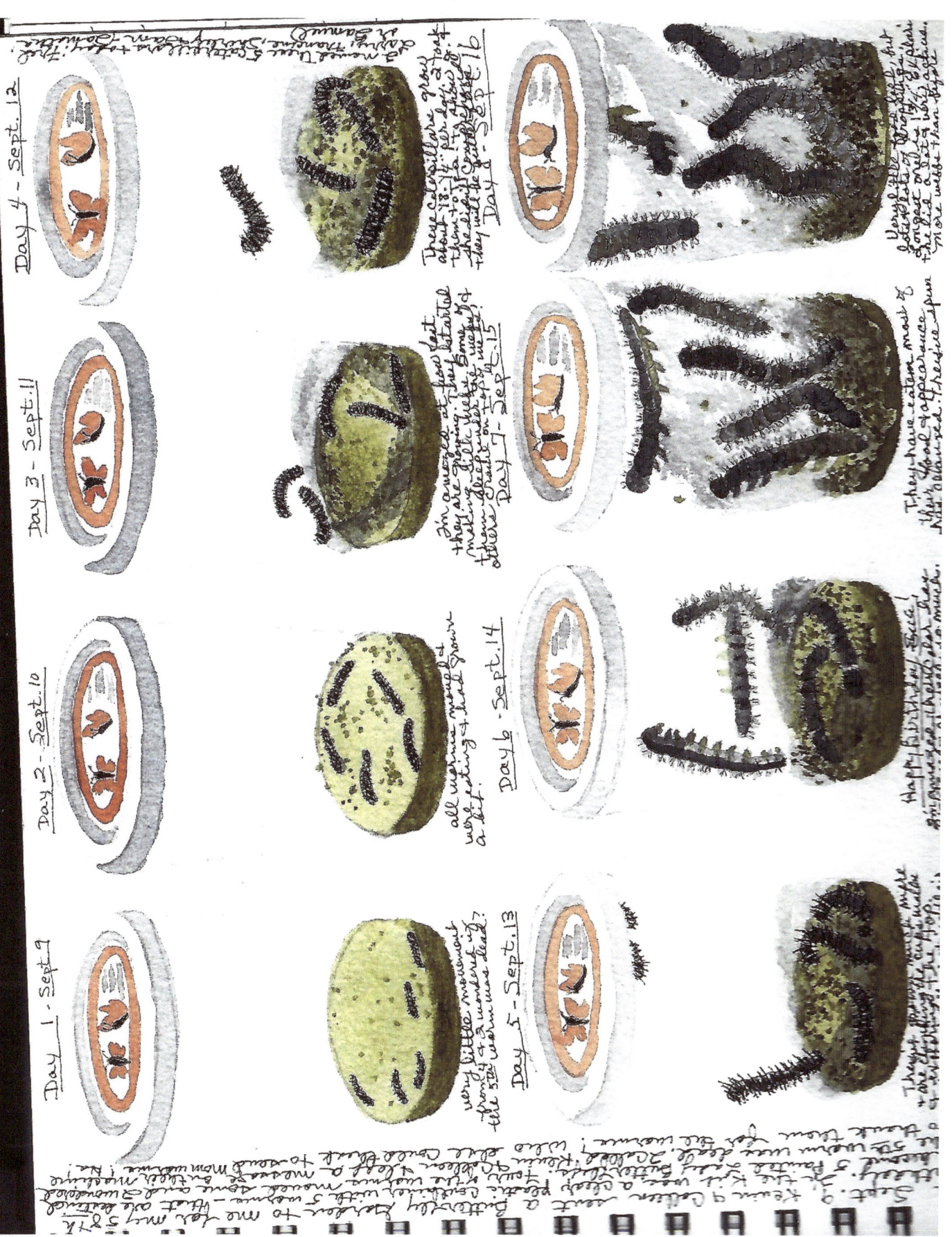

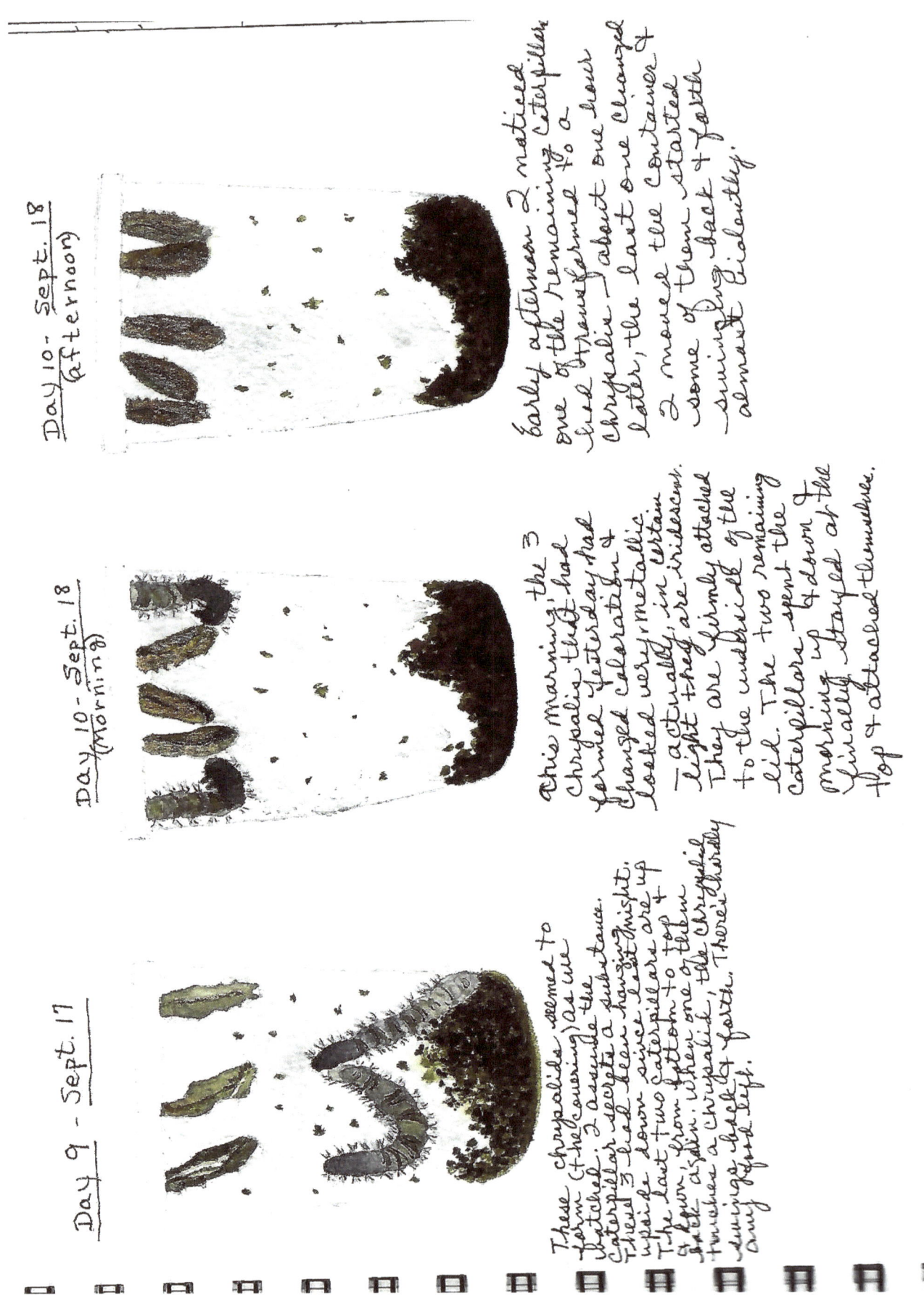

Day 9 - Sept. 17

These chrysalids seemed to form (the covering) as we watched. I would the caterpillar down to a substance they had been having tonight. Their's now six caterpillars are up their's down from bottom to top & side again. When one of them makes a chrysalid, the chrysalid swings back & forth swinging back & forth. Only four left.

Day 10 - Sept. 18 (Morning)

This morning the 3 chrysalids that had formed yesterday had changed color & looked very metallic. Actually, in certain light they are iridescent. They are firmly attached to the underside of the lid. The two remaining caterpillars spent the morning up & down the container. Finally stayed at the top & attached themselves.

Day 10 - Sept. 18 (Afternoon)

Early afternoon I noticed one of the remaining caterpillars had transformed to a live chrysalis. About one hour later, the last one changed & I moved the container. Some of them started swinging back & forth almost violently.

Day 13-16   Sept. 20-24

on Sept. 20, 2 moved the paper with chrysalis attached to the green box. The silk webbing also stuck to the paper & chrysalis. 2 taped paper &abc to the desk of the box.

As the boy was moved or bumped, the chrysalis would swing side to side, sometimes almost violently.

About 8:15 A.M., Sept. 24, Bob & I were talking about the chrysalis & wondering when the butterflies would emerge. I turned my head & Bob said "Look, one is opening." We watched & the butterfly struggled so hard to leave the chrysalis, but I couldn't free himself. It appeared that 1 or 2 strands of silk were holding him. I finally used a pencil to pull the silk away, freeing him—but it was too late, because his wings had already dried & were hopelessly crippled but later proved

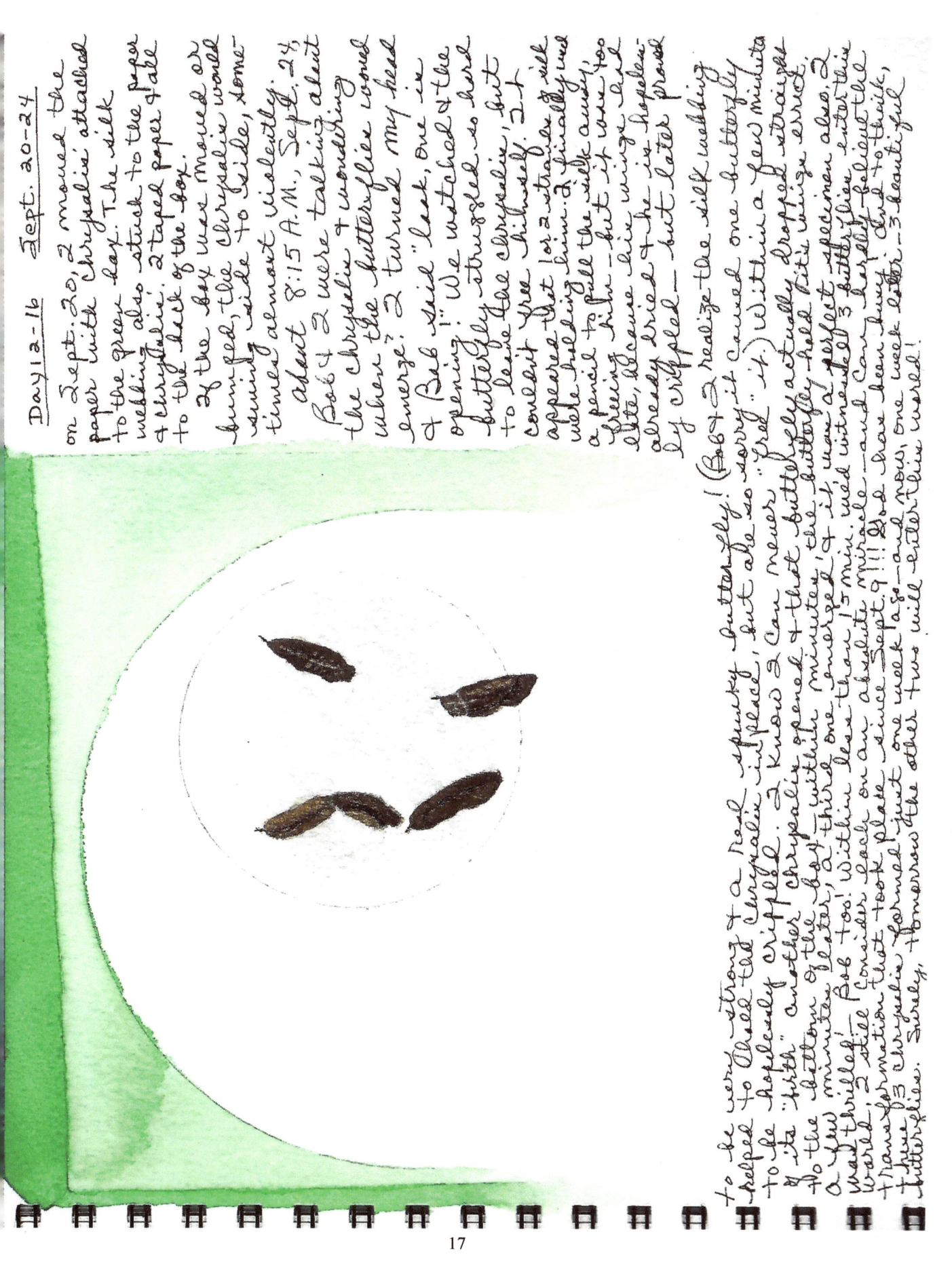

to be very strong & a real spunky butterfly. I felt so sorry it caused one butterfly to be hopelessly crippled, but also so happy to have helped the other. I know I can never "fix" another chrysalis pencil & that butterfly actually dropped straight to the bottom of the box within minutes. The butterfly held his wings erect. a few minutes later, a third one emerged & it was a perfect specimen also. I was thrilled. Bob, too! Within less than 15 min. we'd witnessed 3 butterflies emerging. 2 still come on lack on an adult. Miracle! I hardly believe the transformation that took place since Sept. 9!!! Bob & I have been busy & lived to think these 3 chrysalis formed just one week apart, and now, one week later, 3 beautiful butterflies. Surely, tomorrow the other two will enter this world.

On Sept. 25, about mid-morning, the last two butterflies emerged & are both beautiful & perfect. I asked Meshshake to come up to see them & each one seemed to get a thrill! Bob & I were gone the evening of Sept. 25 & when we got home, two butterflies were mating. We hadn't expected this so soon — later I read that their life span is only 3 weeks. Several times a day 2 went out to put visual water but the leaves & blooms of the lantana, crepe vine, flower & camille will wilt & daisies. They have such flowers & sugar water. I like to watch them uncurl their probosis & eat — just like a long drinking straw. God really is the third one — later two of them were mating. We noticed putting eggs light green spheres on plant leaves on the bottom of the leaf. On many, there were eggs. Many times a day the butterflies flew around & found day window. Desperately trying to escape. On Sept. 28, I taught watercolors to Sarah, Margaret & Lindsey. Our class was about painting butterflies. Brandon Crystal arrived home from "on vacation on Sept 29" She joined us for dinner & later I carried the butterfly lid to the balcony out spread the lid. I assumed the butterflies that were normal would immediately fly away, but they didn't. I had to coax them one at a time. 4th one — places the crippled one stayed in — I few away, so I placed the lid & 2 more of the butterflies returned to the lid. The 4th one was deep inside. The meaning of September 30, Bob & I went for a walk & when we returned, use the day. I labored tiny caterpillars probably crawling in the bottom of the lid. I also crawled out the day onto the rack. They decided caterpillars and also crawled out the day & remaining butterflies & eggs (caterpillars) choice, but to release the two remaining butterflies to the lilacs. I let where I perched too), so I took flowers, but cut off file. The crippled butterfly was perched on the flowers and set them all at once. The other one. Both butterflies the coral vine blossoms, so I placed the butterfly flowers. I for the longest time clinging to & placed them next to the lilacs. Gleanora stayed on the lilacs remained, why the still & started on the strong ones to encourage them to move. I watched them & even the strong wind didn't move. Nature knowing that Finally I felt a strong sense of emptiness mixed with joy, knowing that left a butterflies have two weeks & enjoy the outdoors and we have not & & & I the butterflies have two weeks & one we will never forget had a wonderful experience, — one we will never forget.

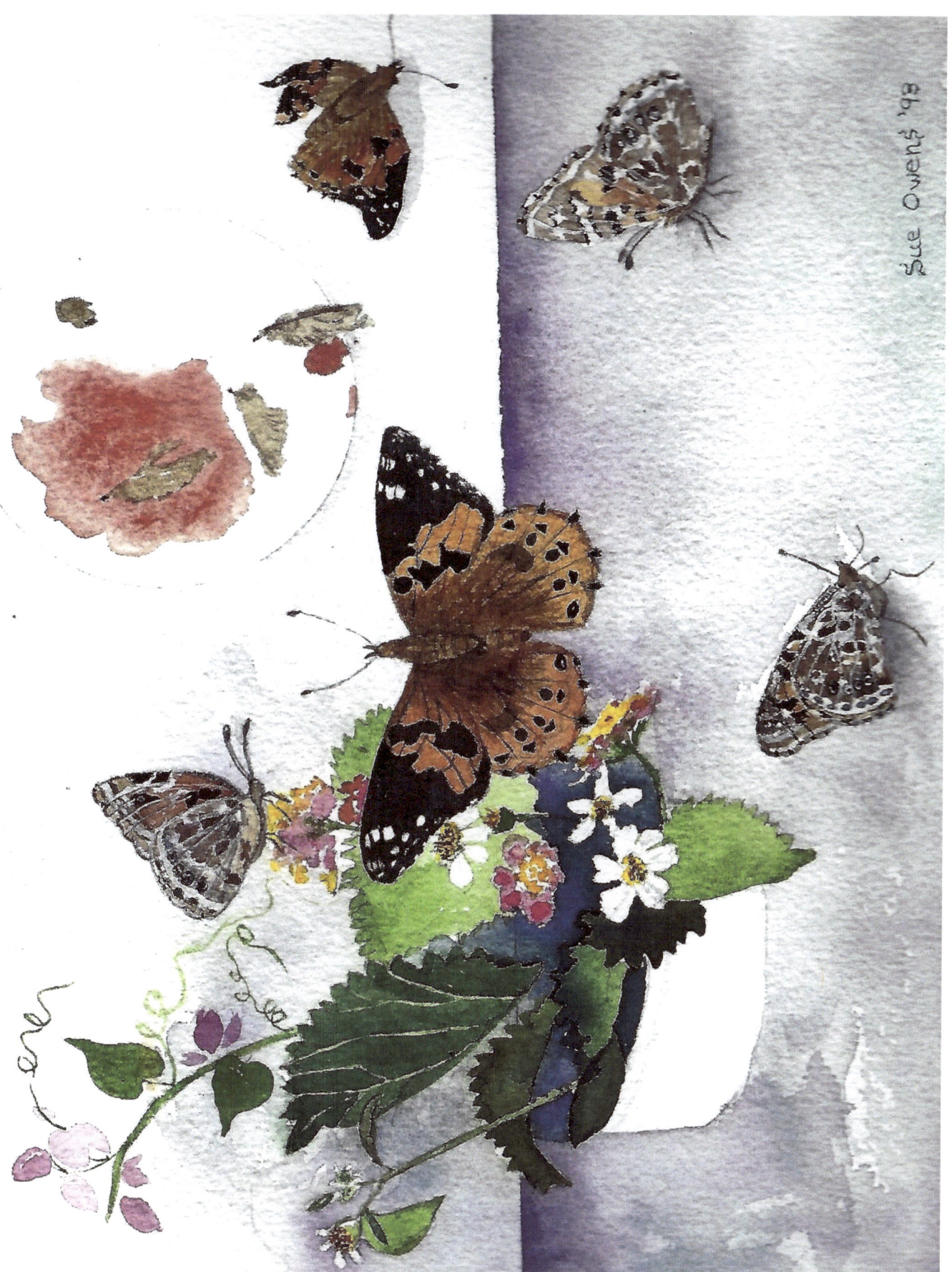

Happiness is a butterfly, which, when pursued, is always just beyond your grasp, but which, if you will sit down quietly, will alight upon you.

Plaque in my kitchen
(Nathaniel Hawthorne quote)

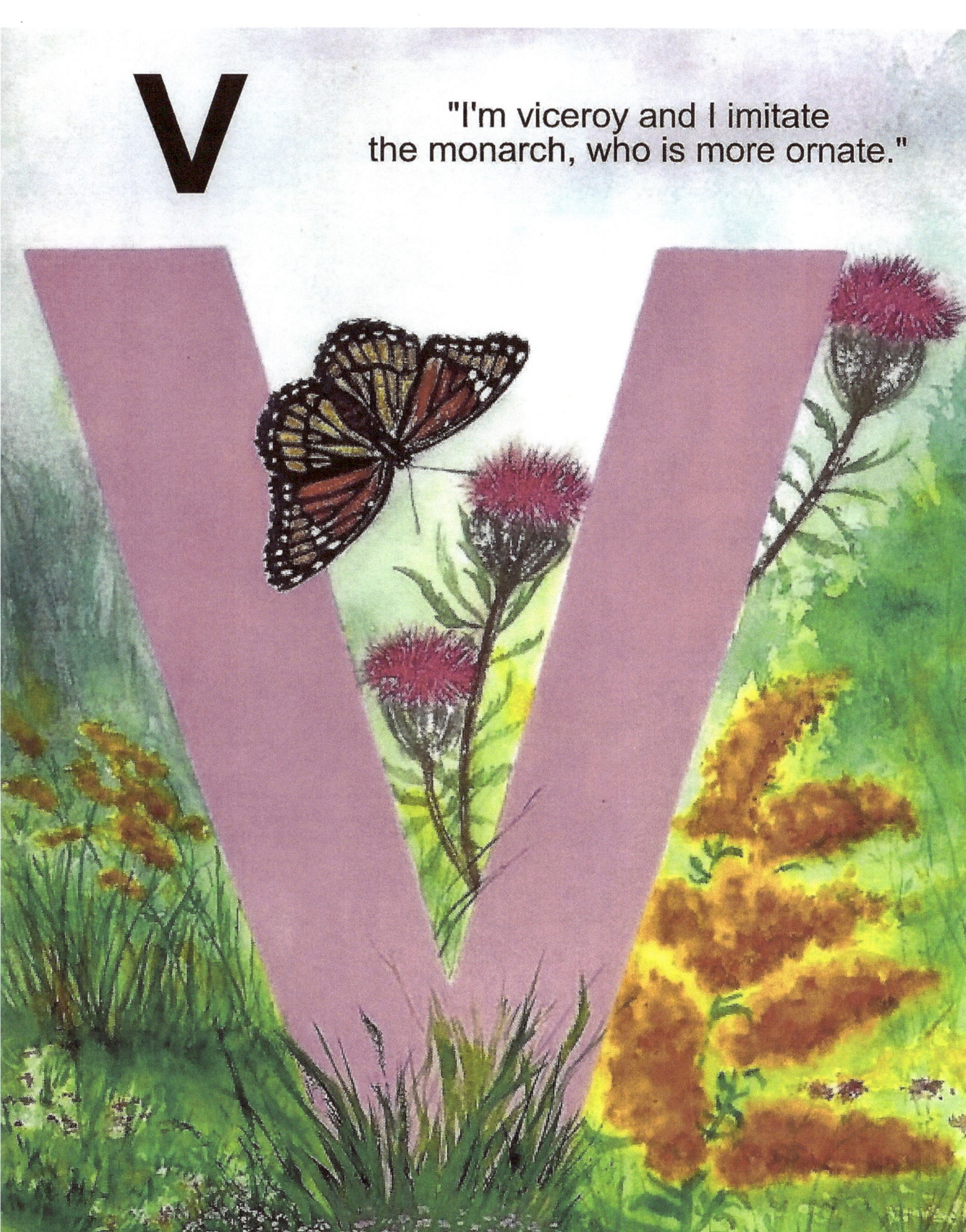

"I'm viceroy and I imitate the monarch, who is more ornate."

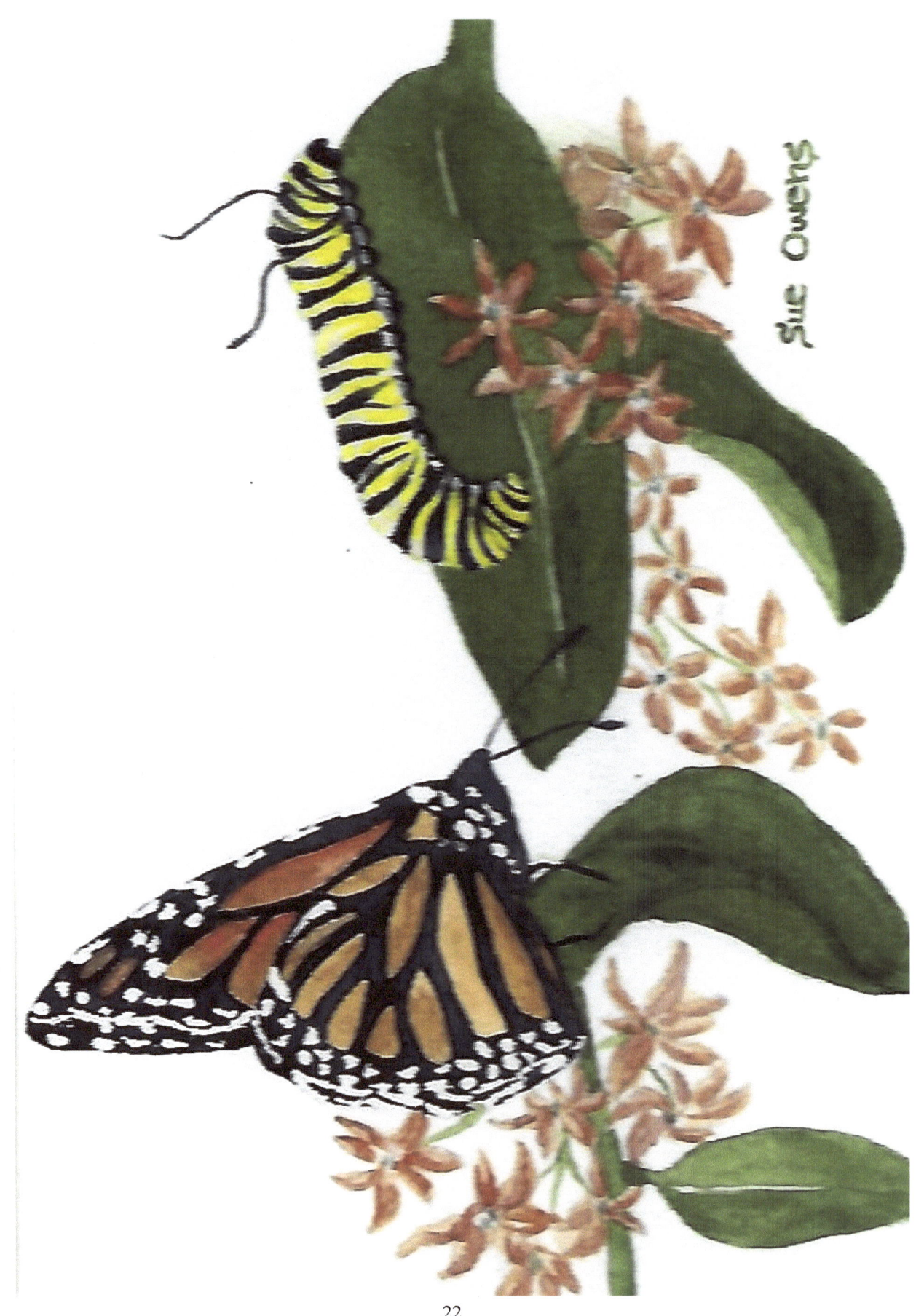

Bob:

I didn't dream how fast the time would fly.
The moments we've shared are like a butterfly.
How can you possibly be seventy-nine?!
Thank God you have a long lifeline!
You'll have a meatloaf dinner on your day
and a glass or two of chardonnay.
Bread pudding, I will plan to bake
instead of the usual birthday cake.
If we have to grow older, I'm glad it's with you.
Happy Birthday, my darling! From your Sweetheart Sue.

       January 17, 2014

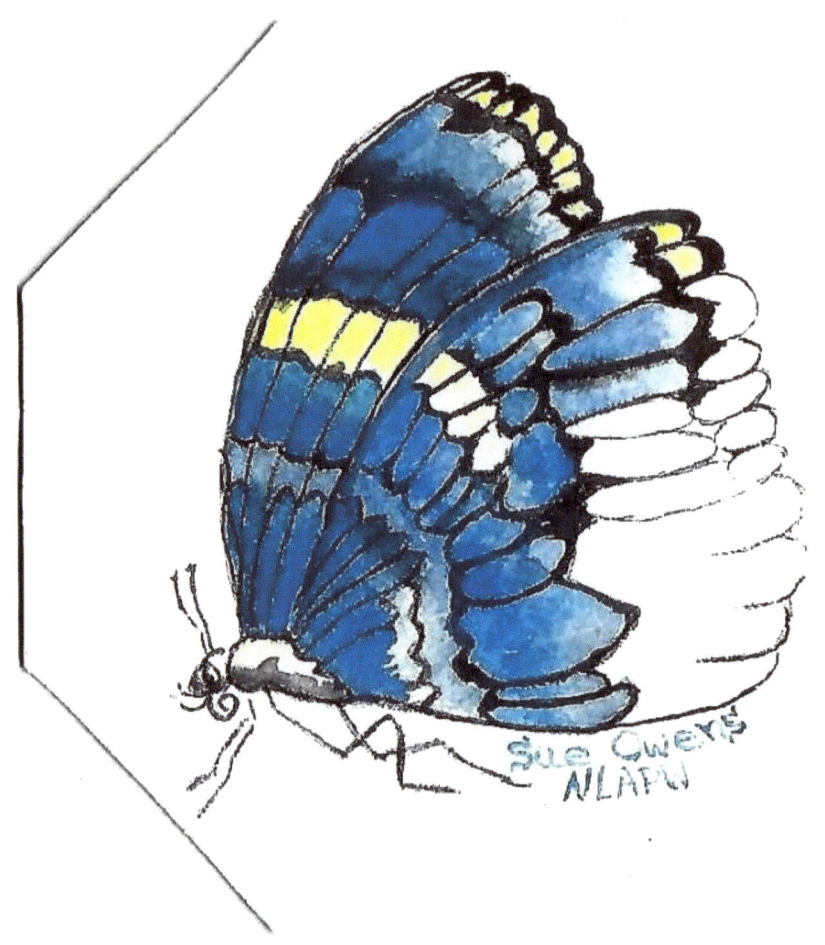

I can't imagine going through life
with anyone else but you.
You're fun, exciting, warm and glowing,
heart-stirring, thrilling — all are true.
Each new year you far surpass
all others with your wealth of class.

Happy Birthday Bob!

Love,
Sue

January 17, 2003

www.ingramcontent.com/pod-product-compliance
Lightning Source LLC
Chambersburg PA
CBHW051836210526
45473CB00005B/1894